PAPER CAPER
Mini Quilts

6 BRIGHT ENGLISH PAPER-PIECED PROJECTS

▶ **Everything You Need** ▶ **No Tracing or Cutting Templates!**

Sue Daley

C&T PUBLISHING

Text, photography, and artwork copyright © 2022 by Sue Daley

Publisher: Amy Barrett-Daffin

Creative Director: Gailen Runge

Acquisitions Editor: Roxane Cerda

Editor: Shannon Mende

Associate Editor: Jennifer Warren

Technical Editor: Gailen Runge

Cover/Book Designer: April Mostek

Production Coordinator: Zinnia Heinzmann

Illustrators: Teresa Williamson and Ashleigh Donovan

Photography Assistant: Gabriel Martinez

Front cover photography by Brooke Duley from Sandpiper Photography

Photography by Brooke Duley from Sandpiper Photography, unless otherwise noted

Published by C&T Publishing, Inc., P.O. Box 1456, Lafayette, CA 94549

Library of Congress Control Number: 2021950778

Printed in China

10 9 8 7 6 5 4 3 2 1

DEDICATED

To my husband Jim

whom I lost suddenly in December 2019.

Jimmy was an encourager and an enabler. He enabled me to follow my passion. He was my biggest fan, and I miss him every day.

To Shannon and Greg

for their endless support.

ACKNOWLEDGMENTS

To my daughter, Shannon, and son-in-law

who work tirelessly, support me, and keep me focused.

To Ashleigh Donovan, my graphic designer

for working alongside of me to make this come to fruition.

To C&T Publishing

for publishing this book.

CONTENTS

Wicklow 15

Shannon 17

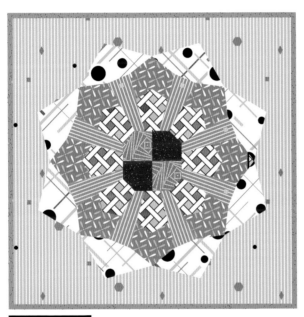

Kinsale 19

Doolin 21

Waterford 23

Cashel 25

INTRODUCTION

This collection has been inspired by my child-hood paper dolls and my current love of small quilts.

What a fabulous combination!

Packaging is also something I love, so being able to store the shapes in their own exclusive little pillow box makes me very happy.

The choice of bright, fun fabrics are from my Colour Wall collection for Riley Blake Designs.

I hope that this collection of small quilts touches your heart the way it has touched mine.

Remember to always enjoy what you do.

THE SUE DALEY ENGLISH PAPER-PIECING GLUE-PEN METHOD

GENERAL REQUIREMENTS

- Popped-out paper shapes

- Size 11 or 15 milliners needles (such as Sue Daley Designs Milliners Needles)

- Glue pen for crafts (such as Sue Daley Designs Sewline Glue Pen)

- Polyester thread (such as Wonderfil DecoBob)

INSTRUCTIONS

These instructions apply to all shapes when paper piecing.

1. Cut the fabric ¼˝ larger than the paper shape all the way around.

2. Lay your fabric right side down and place the paper shape on top (coloured side down), making sure you centre it and glue to the white side of the paper.

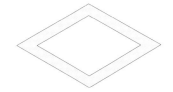

3. Run the glue pen along one side of the paper shape, keeping the glue away from the edge of the paper. Be careful not to take it over the edge onto the fabric (this will cause a buildup, making it difficult to stitch through).

4. Fold the fabric over and hold for a moment. Continue around the shape in one direction until all sides are turned over.

▶ NOTES

- *Don't use too much glue. You will get the hang of it after you have done a few.*

- *In warm weather, the glue can become soft (that is, you will use too much). I suggest putting it in the fridge for a few minutes.*

- *If you use too much glue and the papers are hard to remove, press with a steam iron. The glue will relax, allowing you to remove the papers more easily.*

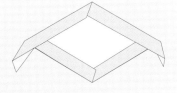

- *Some of the shape's corners will fold in nice and neatly (for example, the hexagon) and others don't (for example, diamonds or pies). See the diagram above. Leave the tails hanging out and make sure that the fabric is nice and tight around the card.*

TO ASSEMBLE THE PIECES

1. Place 2 adjoining pieces right sides together and make a knicker knot (page 8).

2. Whipstitch from corner to corner.

▶ *NOTE Always start with a knicker knot and finish with a knicker knot to secure your thread.*

3. Open the 2 pieces out. With a dry iron, give them a press.

4. Once the mini quilt is completely pieced, remove the paper. Gently peel the fabric back from the papers. The papers can then be reused a number of times.

▶ *NOTES*

- *When sewing stars or pies together, do not sew the tails in. They will automatically lie flat behind your work.*

- *When sewing stars or pies, make sure that you sew 2 halves and then sew them together with 1 seam through the middle. This will eliminate having a hole in the centre of your work.*

- *If you are having problems peeling the fabric back from the paper, you have probably used too much glue. Just dampen slightly with water, which will soften the glue and help you to peel back the fabric.*

VIDEO TUTORIALS

I find it easier to learn from watching someone else. Visit my YouTube channel for video tutorials on my glue-pen method for English paper piecing (for the link, see About the Author, page 32).

THE KNICKER KNOT

The knicker knot starts with thread already through the fabric. If you are continuing stitching but starting a new seam, the thread is already coming up through your material and you're ready to begin the knicker knot.

If you are starting your first stitch line, tie a knot in the end of the thread. Place the 2 fabric pieces right sides together. Run the needle up between the fabric and the card on the wrong side so the needle comes out at the point where you want to start. Do 1 stitch.

1. Bring the needle around to the back (essentially taking a whipstitch). Pass the needle through all layers of fabric, but stop with the needle in your work. You will have a thread at the front of your work and 2 threads coming out the eye of the needle.

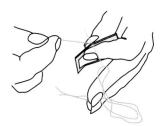

2. Take the single thread and pass it under the needle to the left.

3. Take the double thread and do the opposite—pass it to the right side of the needle. Wrap underneath and around the needle.

4. Pull the thread through to create the knot.

5. If the threads don't make a knot, you have wrapped both threads in the same direction.

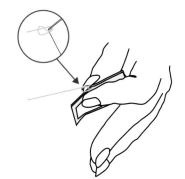

FINISHING INSTRUCTIONS

LAYER THE QUILT

Option 1: Spray Baste

1. Lay the backing on a table with the wrong side facing up, and tape it down. Spray sparingly with spray baste.

2. Lay the wadding (batting) on top and spray lightly.

3. With the right side up, lay the top onto the wadding. Smooth out with your hand and press.

Option 2: Pinning or Tacking

1. Lay the backing on a table with the wrong side facing up, and tape it down.

2. Lay the wadding (batting) on top.

3. With the right side up, lay the top onto the wadding.

4. Pin or thread baste all 3 layers together.

▶ **NOTE** *These instructions are not required if you are having your quilt professionally quilted.*

QUILTING

1. Quilt in your preferred manner, either by yourself or by a professional.

2. Trim up the quilt top.

BINDING

1. The binding is made from 2″-wide strips. Join the strips end to end and press the seams open.

2. Fold the binding in half lengthwise with wrong sides together and press.

3. Line up the raw edge of the binding with the edge of the quilt, right sides together.

4. Start stitching partway along one side, leaving about 6″ of binding loose at the beginning.

5. Mitre each of the corners as you go, following the diagrams below.

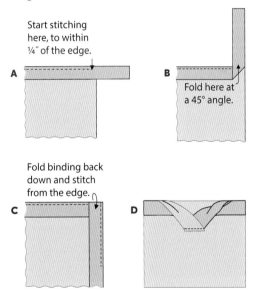

6. When you get to within approximately 6″ of the end, remove from the machine.

7. Measure and join the binding pieces together. Continue to sew the remaining binding to the quilt. Once you have finished, fold the binding over to the back and hand sew with a slip stitch.

APPLIQUÉ INSTRUCTIONS

▶ NOTE *If you are using cotton thread, then the thread should match the colour of the appliqué pieces. If they don't always match, go a shade darker rather than lighter.*

▶ HINT *I use Wonderfil DecoBob thread for appliqué, as it is fine and strong, and it blends, eliminating the need to have copious amounts of different coloured threads.*

TRADITIONAL NEEDLE-TURN APPLIQUÉ

1. Trace around the template with a fabric pencil, such as Sewline Fabric Pencil, onto the right side of the fabric.

2. Cut out each piece with a scant ¼″ seam allowance.

3. Place the piece onto the background fabric and glue (I use Sue Daley Designs Appliqué Glue) or pin into position.

4. Using a milliners needle size 11, size 15 (if you prefer a longer needle), or size 10 (if you need a larger eye), turn the seam allowance under little by little and sew with an appliqué stitch.

▶ NOTE *Sometimes there is an order of placement, in which case you need to follow the placement in number order.*

APPLIQUÉING EPP SHAPES TO A BACKGROUND

1. Press your blocks well.

2. Remove the papers.

3. Press again.

4. Using a small amount of appliqué glue, baste the block into position.

5. Because the edges of the pieces are already folded under, you can go ahead and sew the pieces in place with an appliqué stitch (see technique below). Remember to always start on the straightest edge where possible.

▶ NOTE *If you are right-handed, sew from right to left across the top of your work. If you are left-handed, sew from left to right across the top of your work.*

Applique Stitch

1. Knot your thread. Bring the needle up from the back of your work into the fold line, and lose the knot in the seam allowance.

2. Go straight down into the background fabric nice and close to the fold line.

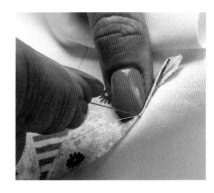

3. Come up on an angle, and pick up a couple of threads of fabric in the fold.

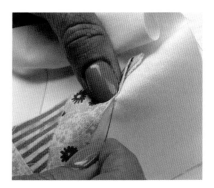

4. Go straight back down into the background fabric nice and close to where your thread is coming out of the fold.

5. Continue in this manner until you get to the end.

APPLIQUÉING POINTS WITH TAILS

I treat these just like I am doing traditional needle-turn appliqué, but instead of a drawn line I have a fold line to work to.

1. Pull the seam allowance out from underneath the shape.

2. Fold under the edge that you are working on right up to the point. Sew right to the point.

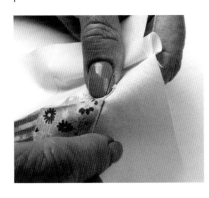

3. Turn your work around and put a stitch into the very point.

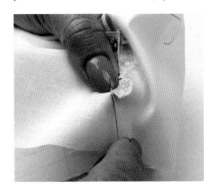

4. You might see a little tail poking out from underneath your seam allowance. Lift up the seam allowance and trim a little off the tail.

5. Come back and trim the seam allowance back to 3/16˝. (This only needs to be trimmed near the point.)

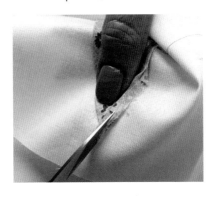

6. Do another stitch right at the point.

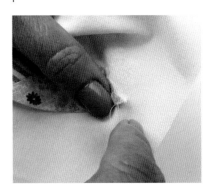

7. Use your needle to ease the fabric under, and sew as you go.

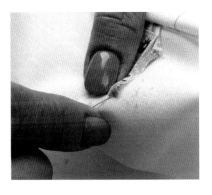

Try not to poke at the fabric point too much with the point of your needle, as you will only fray your fabric. Continue sewing along the edge.

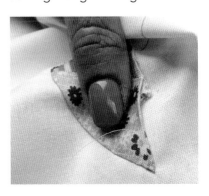

TOOLS

SUE DALEY FABRIC GLUE PEN

I swear by this product so much I put my name on it! The Sue Daley Fabric Glue Pen (by Sewline) is a water-soluble pink glue that dries clear. Save time basting your English paper pieces and use the glue pen instead of basting stitches. This will cut your preparation time at least in half.

SUE DALEY DESIGNS MILLINERS NEEDLES

These needles are beautiful to use. The milliners needles are long and fine with a nice, big gold eye, which makes it easier to thread.

This needle is perfect for everyone but especially for those who suffer from arthritis or carpal tunnel or for those who have long fingernails. Because the needle is long, there is no need to grip it tightly, therefore eliminating any pain in your hand that you may experience.

Sizes 11 and 15 are the most popular for English paper piecing and needle-turn appliqué (the larger the size number, the finer the needle).

Available in sizes 7, 9, 10, 11, and 15

If you prefer a larger eye, I recommend size 9 or 10; these are also used for wool appliqué.

SUE DALEY DESIGNS ROTATING CUTTING MAT

The 10″ and 16″ Sue Daley Designs pink rotating cutting mats are a must-have accessory for English paper piecing and are especially useful for patchworkers on the move. This rotary board is perfect for trimming up your blocks, half-square triangles, cutting and gluing your English paper-piecing shapes, and auditioning your quilt blocks. It is also a beautiful accessory for your sewing room.

SUE DALEY DESIGNS APPLIQUÉ GLUE

The Sue Daley Designs Appliqué Glue now comes in a new and improved bottle with a soft squeeze and pointed nib for accurate application. It's just like having liquid pins! This product is fantastic for needle-turn appliqué. A single 30ml bottle will last for years.

SUE DALEY DESIGNS FUSSY CUTTING MIRROR

This convenient little tool is very handy for any patchworker! This mirror is 5½″ × 5½″ and allows you to see how a block will look when fussy cut. Simply place the mirror on your fabric over the piece you wish to fussy cut!

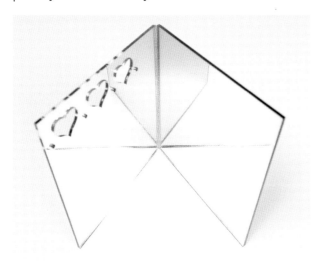

SUE DALEY DESIGNS WONDERFIL BOBBINATOR

Wonderfil DecoBob is the perfect thread for all of your English paper-piecing and needle-turn appliqué needs. It is strong and will withstand the constant dragging over the card when English paper piecing. It is also fine, allowing your stitches to disappear into your work so they become invisible. It works perfectly with the Sue Daley Designs milliners needles.

The Bobbinator is designed to turn your bobbin into a spool of thread! It is a practical and convenient way to carry your English paper-piecing thread without getting tangles. Each Bobbinator will fit a total of 4 bobbins. Each pack includes 10 prewound 80-weight cottonised polyester thread on plastic bobbins and your very own Bobbinator.

SUE DALEY DESIGNS LITTLE KEEPER

The Little Keeper makes it simple to keep everything you need for English paper piecing and handwork within easy reach, at home or on the go. Keep your needle secure on the powerful embedded magnet, use the pen slot for quick access to your Sue Daley Fabric Glue Pen while paper piecing, and stow your thread on the removable bobbin holder for effortless and tangle-free sewing.

This Little Keeper is ¾″ × 3½″ and is sure to be your constant companion wherever your stitching takes you.

OLFA ROTARY CUTTERS

OLFA rotary cutters are a necessity for any patchworker! They are easy to use with replaceable blades. OLFA rotary cutters are available in both regular and ergonomic designs and come in 4 sizes: 18mm, 28mm, 45mm, and 60mm.

ACRYLIC TEMPLATE SETS

Optional template sets are available to purchase separately for each of the 6 projects.

PAPER CAPER
Wicklow

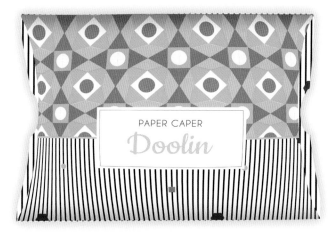

PAPER CAPER
Doolin

PAPER CAPER
Shannon

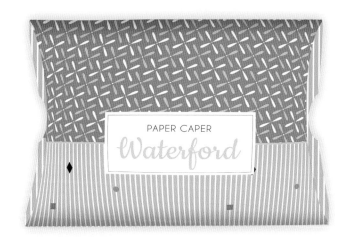

PAPER CAPER
Waterford

PAPER CAPER
Kinsale

PAPER CAPER
Cashel

WICKLOW

Finished size: 14″ × 14″

General Requirements

- Fat eighth of 8 assorted fabrics for EPP
- Fat eighth of white fabric for EPP
- Fat eighth of 2 pinks for EPP and appliqué
- 15cm (¼ yd) of fabric for binding

Cutting Instructions

For all shapes, cut the fabric ¼″ larger than the shape all the way around, following the instructions in The Sue Daley English Paper-Piecing Glue-Pen Method (page 7).

> ▶ **NOTE** *Cut all shapes and lay them out to make sure they are going in the same direction before sewing.*

From each of the 8 coloured fabrics

- 6 of shape A

From the white fabric

- 16 each of shapes B, C, and D

From each of the 2 pink fabrics

- 8 of shape E
- 2 circles

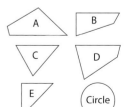

CONSTRUCTION

Follow the instructions in The Sue Daley English Paper-Piecing Glue-Pen Method (page 7) and Appliqué Instructions (page 10) to complete the quilt.

> ▶ **NOTE** *When glueing the shapes for the outside edge, always glue the outside edges last, as ¼˝ will be needed for you to sew the binding to.*

1. Push out the papers from the Wicklow pages.

2. Following the illustration for fabric placement, make the following combinations for 1 block in the quilt: 4 C/A, 4 B/A, 4 D/A.

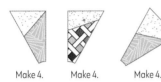

Make 4.   Make 4.   Make 4.

3. Sew all 3 together into a set.

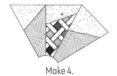

Make 4.

4. Sew the 4 sets together.

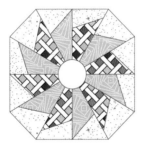

5. Appliqué the circle to the centre.

> ▶ **NOTE** *This can also be done last.*

6. Sew the corners of the block.

7. Repeat Steps 2–6 to make 4 blocks, and sew the 4 blocks together.

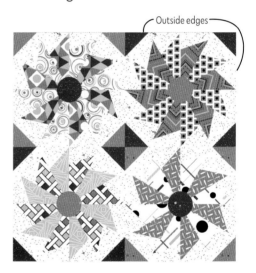

Outside edges

8. Remove the papers. Press. Fold the edges out.

9. Follow Finishing Instructions (page 9) to finish the mini quilt.

SHANNON

Finished size: 14″ × 14″

General Requirements

- Fat eighth of 6 assorted solid fabrics for EPP
- Fat quarter of white fabric for EPP
- 15cm (¼ yd) of fabric for binding

Cutting Instructions

For all shapes, cut the fabric ¼″ larger than the shape all the way around following the instructions in The Sue Daley English Paper-Piecing Glue-Pen Method (page 7).

From the white fabric
- 45 of shape A
- 14 of shape C
- 8 of shape D

From the solid fabrics, cut the following number of shape B
- 16 purple
- 18 pale pink
- 21 green
- 14 dark pink
- 19 yellow
- 16 blue

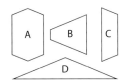

CONSTRUCTION

Follow the instructions in The Sue Daley English Paper-Piecing Glue-Pen Method (page 7) to complete the quilt.

> **▶NOTE** *When glueing the shapes for the outside edge, always glue the outside edges last, as ¼˝ will be needed for you to sew the binding to.*

1. Push out the papers from the Shannon pages.

2. Follow the illustration for colour placement and sew the B-A-B units (making 8 green, 6 blue, 7 yellow, 8 purple, 9 pale pink, and 7 dark pink) and A-C units (making 5 yellow, 5 green, and 4 blue).

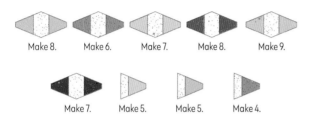

3. Join the units together in rows, as shown in the diagram.

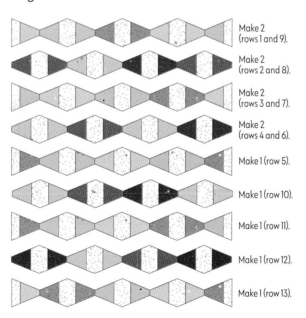

4. Join the rows together.

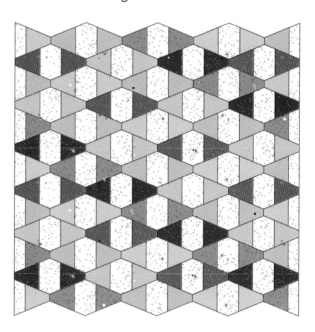

5. Sew the white D pieces to the top and bottom.

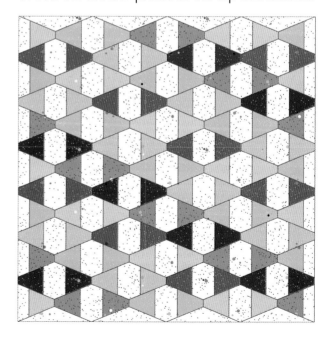

6. Press. Remove the papers. Unfold all of the edges and press.

7. Follow Finishing Instructions (page 9) to finish the mini quilt.

KINSALE

Finished size: 14″ × 14″

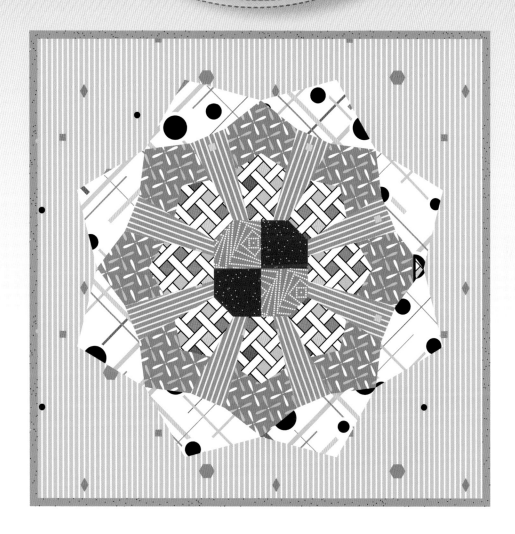

General Requirements

- Fat eighth of 6 assorted fabrics for EPP (dark pink, light pink, multicoloured check, blue print, grey stripe, and white print)

- 15″ × 15″ square background fabric (to be trimmed to 14½″ × 14½″ after appliqué)

- 15cm (¼ yd) for binding

Cutting Instructions

For all shapes, cut the fabric ¼″ larger than the shape all the way around following the instructions in The Sue Daley English Paper-Piecing Glue-Pen Method (page 7).

From the dark pink fabric
- 2 of shape A

From the light pink fabric
- 2 of shape A

From the multicoloured checked fabric
- 4 of shape B
- 4 of shape E

From the blue print fabric
- 8 of shape C
- 8 of shape CR

From the grey stripe fabric
- 4 of shape D
- 4 of shape DR

From the white print fabric
- 8 of shape F

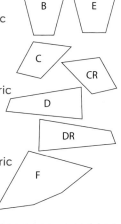

CONSTRUCTION

Follow the instructions in The Sue Daley English Paper-Piecing Glue-Pen Method (page 7) and Appliqué Instructions (page 10) to complete the quilt.

1. Push out the papers from the Kinsale pages.

2. Follow the illustration for colour placement and sew the following pairs:

  2 A-A pairs with a light pink and a dark pink

  8 C-CR pairs

3. Sew the pairs from Step 2 into larger units as follows:

  1 A-A-A-A unit

  4 B-C-CR units

  4 E-C-CR units

4. Sew a D and a DR to either side of the B-C-CR unit.

Make 2.   Make 1.

Make 8 pairs.   Make 4.   Make 4.

Make 4.

5. Join the pieces to the centre octagon.

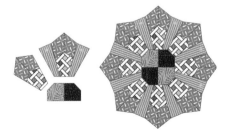

6. Join the outside pieces. Press.

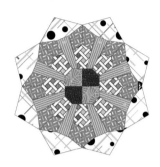

7. Take the 15˝ square, fold it in half and in quarters, and press to find the centre.

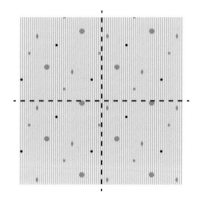

8. Remove the papers, and glue baste the EPP block into position in the centre of the background using appliqué glue. Appliqué the edge of the block to the background.

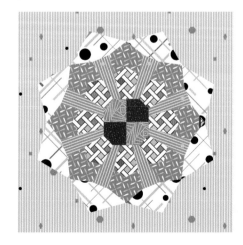

9. Press. Trim the block back to 14½˝ × 14½˝.

10. Follow Finishing Instructions (page 9) to finish the mini quilt.

DOOLIN

Finished size: 14″ × 14″

General Requirements

- Fat eighth of 7 assorted fabrics for EPP (white, multicoloured print, blue, orange, grey, stripe, and green)
- 15cm (¼ yd) of fabric for binding

Cutting Instructions

For all shapes, cut the fabric ¼″ larger than the shape all the way around following instructions in The Sue Daley English Paper-Piecing Glue-Pen Method (page 7).

From the white fabric
- 32 of shape A

From the multicoloured fabric
- 4 of shape A

From the blue fabric
- 12 of shape B

From the orange fabric
- 20 of shape B

From the grey fabric
- 4 of shape B

From the stripe fabric
- 16 of shape C

From the green fabric
- 8 of shape D

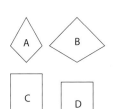

CONSTRUCTION

Follow the instructions in The Sue Daley English Paper-Piecing Glue-Pen Method (page 7) and Appliqué Instructions (page 10) to complete the quilt.

▶ **NOTE** *When glueing the shapes for the outside edge, always glue the outside edges last, as ¼˝ will be needed for you to sew the binding to.*

1. Push out the papers from the Doolin pages.

2. Follow the illustration for colour placement and sew the following units:

1 unit with 4 multicoloured fabric As and 4 grey Bs

4 units with 4 white As, 3 orange Bs, and 1 blue B

4 units with 4 white As, 2 orange Bs, and 2 blue Bs

8 D/C units

4 C/C units

3. Follow the illustration to make 4 corners and 1 centre.

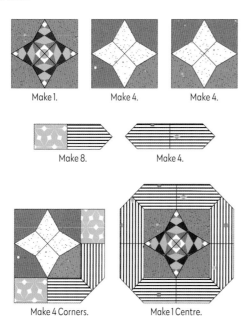

Make 1. Make 4. Make 4.

Make 8. Make 4.

Make 4 Corners. Make 1 Centre.

4. Join pieces together in rows as shown in the diagram.

Edge pieces

5. Press. Remove papers. Fold out the edges of the quilt and press.

6. Follow Finishing Instructions (page 9) to finish the mini quilt.

WATERFORD

Finished size: 14″ × 14″

General Requirements

- Fat eighth of 8 assorted fabrics for EPP (green print, pink print, black stripe, light blue, dark blue, white, yellow, and pink)

- 15″ × 15″ square of background fabric (to be trimmed back to 14½″ × 14½″ after appliqué)

- 15cm (¼ yd) of fabric for binding

Cutting Instructions

For all shapes, cut the fabric ¼″ larger than the shape all the way around following instructions in The Sue Daley English Paper-Piecing Glue-Pen Method (page 7).

From green print fabric
- 9 of shape B

From pink pin fabric
- 9 of shape B

From black stripe fabric
- 18 of shape B

From light and dark blue fabric
- 3 of shape B each

From white fabric
- 18 of shape BR

From yellow and pink fabric
- 9 of shape A each

CONSTRUCTION

*Follow the instructions in The Sue Daley English Paper-Piecing Glue-Pen Method (page 7)
and Appliqué Instructions (page 10) to complete the quilt.*

1. Push out the papers from the Waterford pages.

2. Follow the illustration for colour placement
and sew the following:

3 blocks with 3 pink print and 3 black stripe Bs

3 blocks with 3 green print and 3 black stripe Bs

1 block with 3 light blue and 3 dark blue Bs

3 blocks with 3 white BRs and 3 yellow As

3 blocks with 3 white BRs and 3 pink As

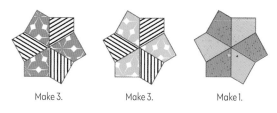

Make 3.   Make 3.   Make 1.

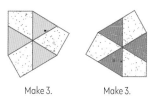

Make 3.   Make 3.

3. Join all the pieces together to match the
illustration. Press.

4. Take the background fabric and fold it in half
and in quarters to find the centre.

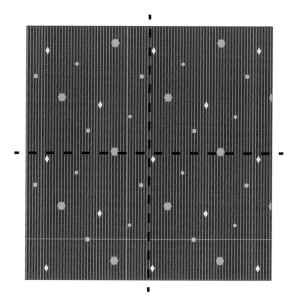

5. Remove the papers and glue baste the block
to the background. Appliqué the edges. Press.

6. Trim back to 14½˝ × 14½˝.

7. Follow Finishing Instructions (page 9) to finish
the mini quilt.

CASHEL

Finished size: 14˝ × 14˝

General Requirements

- Fat eighth of 10 assorted fabrics for EPP (dotted grey, dotted white, white print, dotted blue, yellow print, light pink print, dark pink print, green print, blue stripe, and grey stripe)

- 15cm (⅛ yd) of fabric for binding

Cutting Instructions

For all shapes, cut the fabric ¼˝ larger than the shape all the way around following instructions in The Sue Daley English Paper-Piecing Glue-Pen Method (page 7).

From the dotted grey fabric
- 5 of shape A

From the dotted white fabric
- 4 of shape A
- 16 of shape BR
- 16 of shape CR

From the white print fabric
- 20 of shape B
- 20 of shape C

From the dotted blue fabric
- 20 of shape BR
- 20 of shape CR

From the bright prints (yellow, light pink, dark pink, and green) fabrics
- 4 of shape B from each fabric
- 4 of shape C from each fabric

From the blue stripe fabric
- 40 of shape D

From the grey stripe fabric
- 32 of shape D

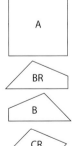

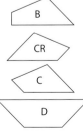

CONSTRUCTION

Follow the instructions in The Sue Daley English Paper-Piecing Glue-Pen Method (page 7) and Appliqué Instructions (page 10) to complete the quilt.

> ▶ **NOTE** *When glueing the shapes for the outside edge, always glue the outside edges last, as ¼″ will be needed for you to sew the binding to.*

1. Push out the papers from the Cashel pages.

2. Follow the illustrations for colour placement and prepare the following units for each blue block (keeping the dotted grey As handy for Step 4):

Make 4 units with a white print B and dotted blue BR; then add a dotted blue CR and a white print C to the outsides.

Make 4. / Make 4 reversed. / Make 4. / Make 4 reversed.

Make 4 units with 2 blue stripe Ds.

Make 1. / Make 4. / Make 4.

3. Follow the illustrations for colour placement and prepare the following units for each bright print block (keeping the dotted white As handy for Step 4):

Make 4 units with a bright print B and a dotted white BR; then add a dotted white CR and a bright print C to the outsides.

Make 4. / Make 4 reversed. / Make 4. / Make 4 reversed.

Make 4 units with 2 grey stripe Ds.

Make 1. / Make 4. / Make 4.

4. Join the CR-B-BR-C units and the A shape together for each of 5 blue blocks and 4 bright print blocks.

Make 5. / Make 4 in assorted colours.

5. Add the corners.

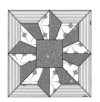

Make 5. / Make 4.

6. Join the blocks together in rows. Press.

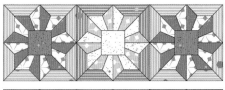
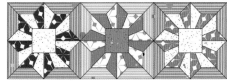
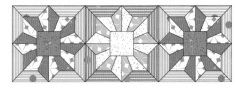

7. Join the rows together. Press.

8. Remove papers. Fold out the edges and press.

9. Follow Finishing Instructions (page 9) to finish the mini quilt.

BONUS
DESIGNS

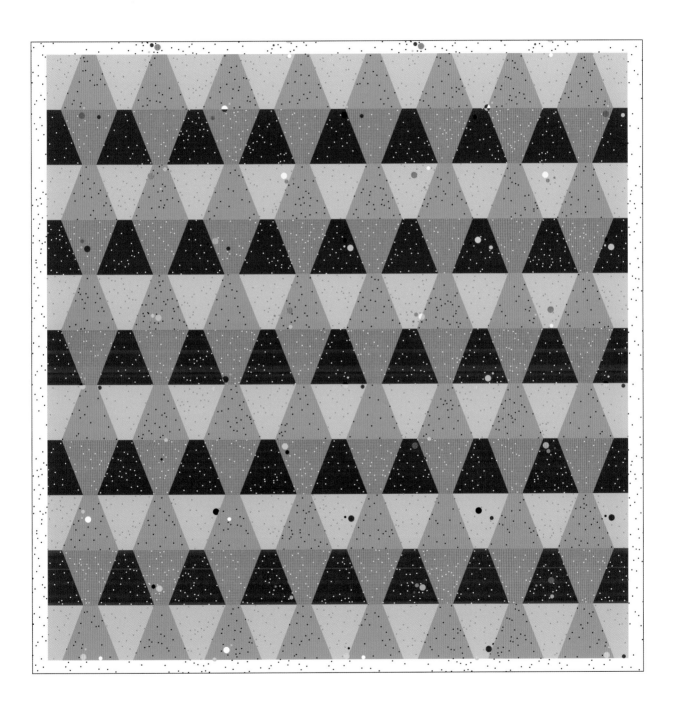

Finished size: Approximately 14″ × 14″

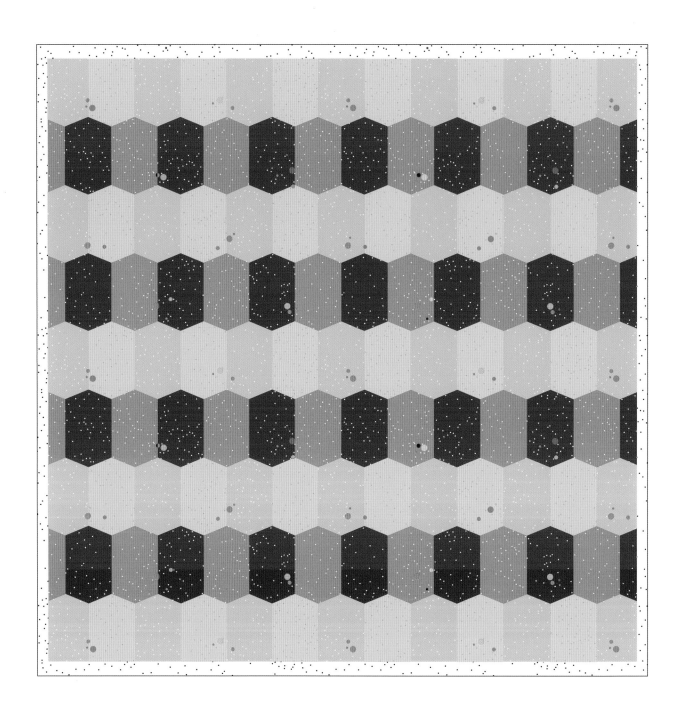

Finished size: Approximately 14″ × 14″

QUILT DESIGN INSPIRATION

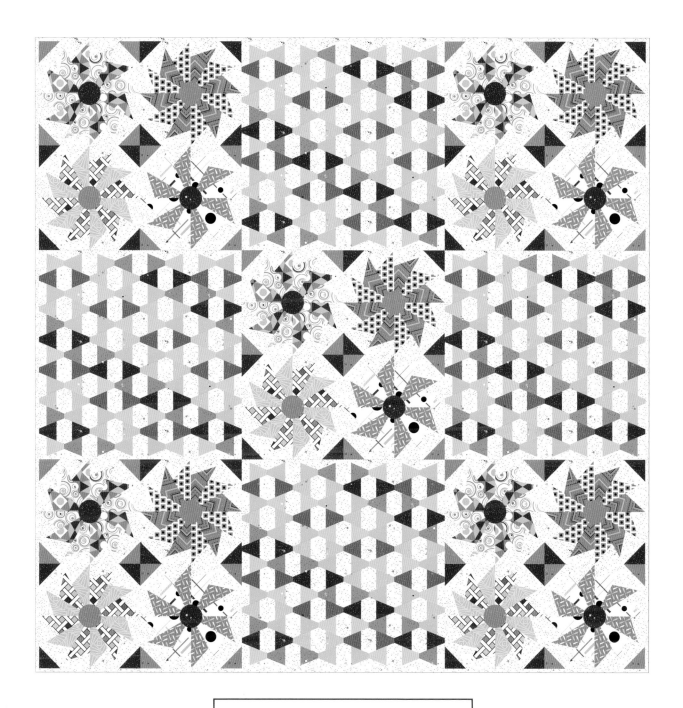

Wicklow and Shannon

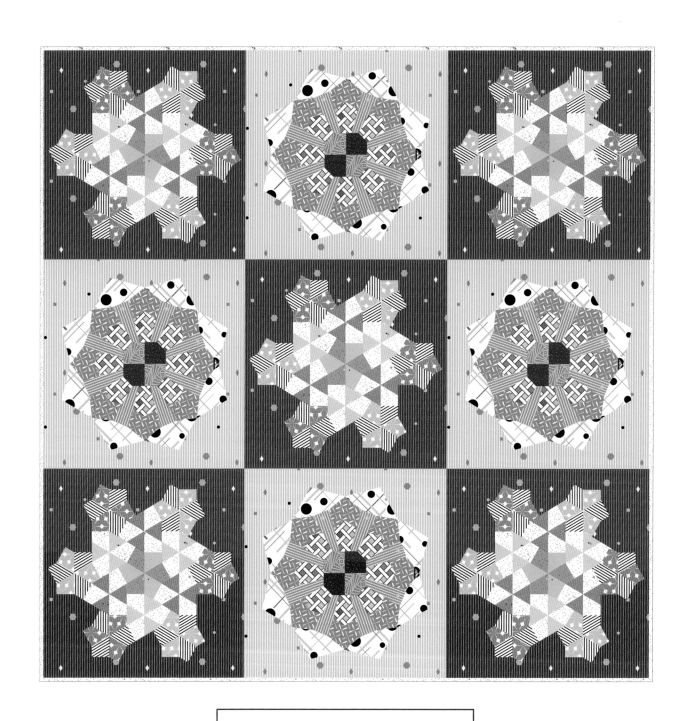

Kinsale and Waterford

Wicklow and Cashel

ABOUT THE AUTHOR

Sue Daley was born and raised in the South-Eastern suburbs of Sydney, Australia.

She worked for many years as a detail draftsperson, but her love of fabric and design was so great that she eventually turned it into a successful business.

By streamlining the English paper piecing technique, Sue was able to make it more user friendly for everyone.

She now lives on the beautiful Sunshine Coast, where she spends time on her passion of patchwork and designing.

Follow Sue on social media!

YouTube: /suedaleydesigns

See video tutorials about Sue's English paper-piecing method, using Sue Daley Designs tools, and more!

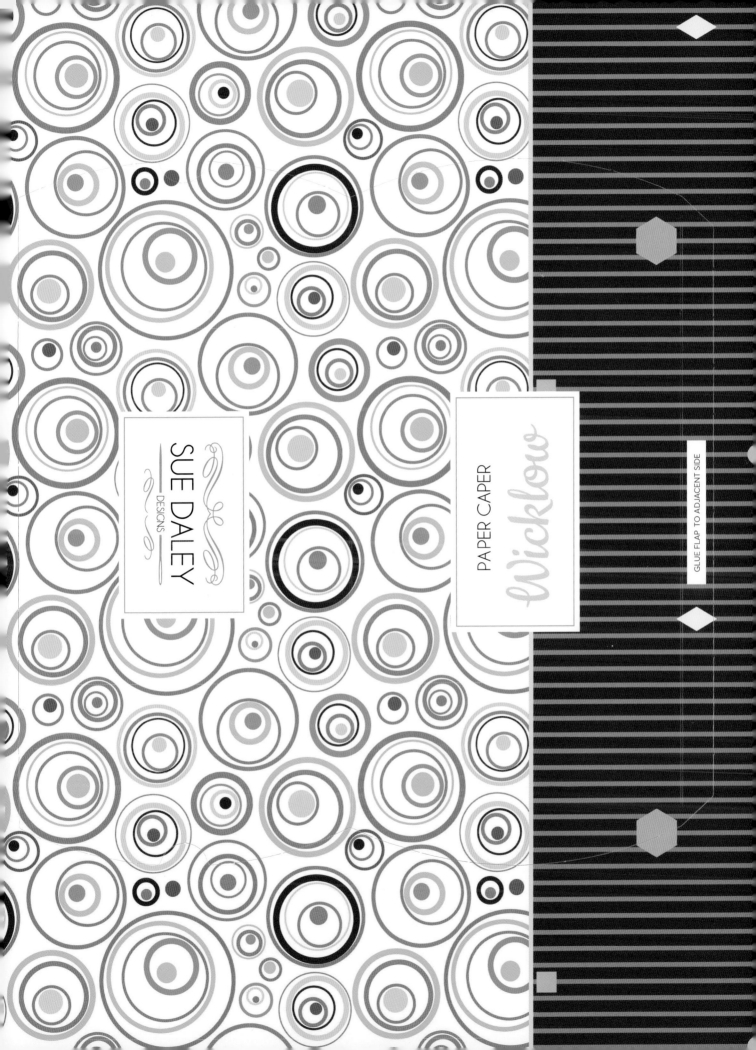

SUE DALEY
DESIGNS

PAPER CAPER
Wicklow

GLUE FLAP TO ADJACENT SIDE

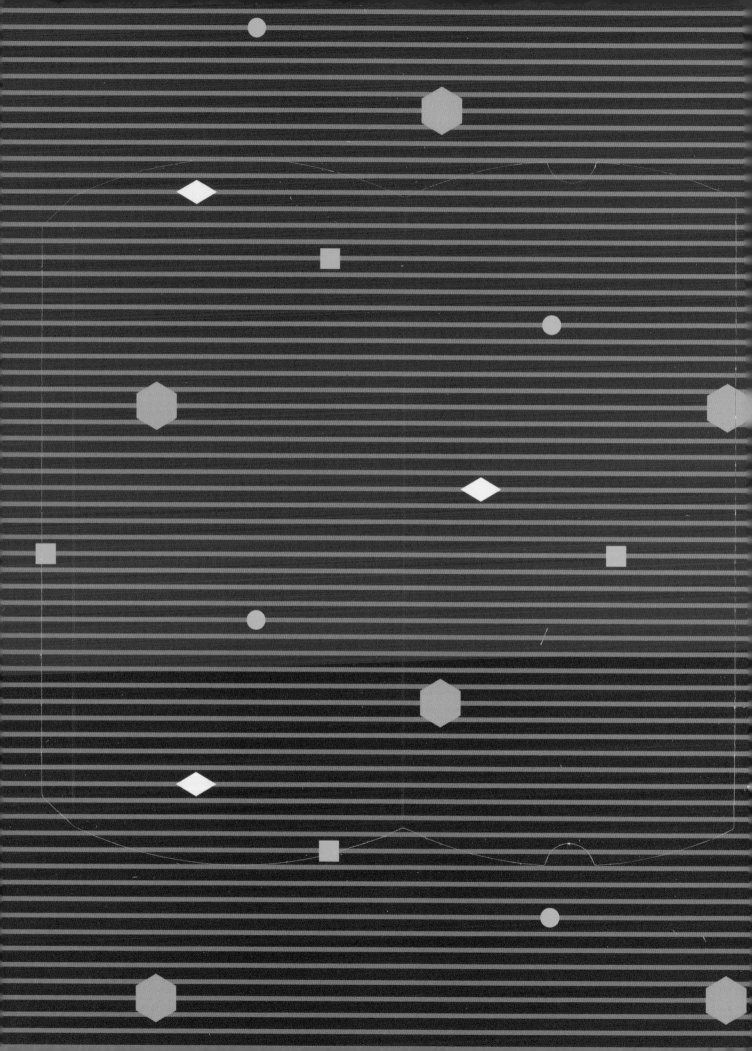

SUE DALEY
DESIGNS

PAPER CAPER
Shannon

GLUE FLAP TO ADJACENT SIDE

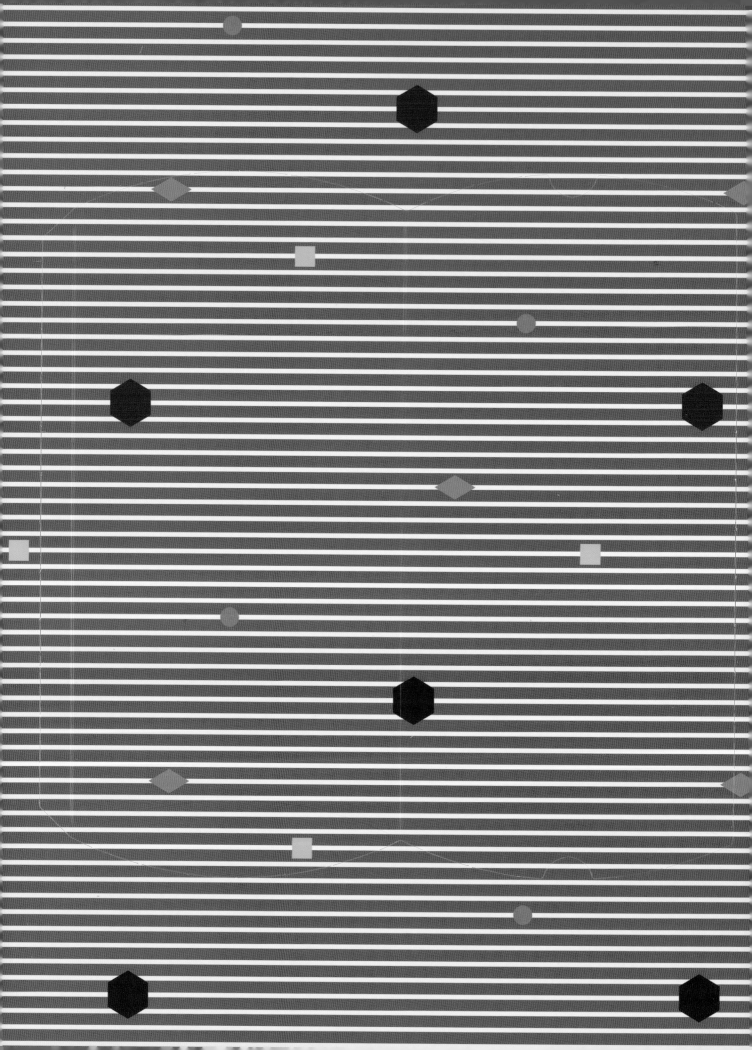

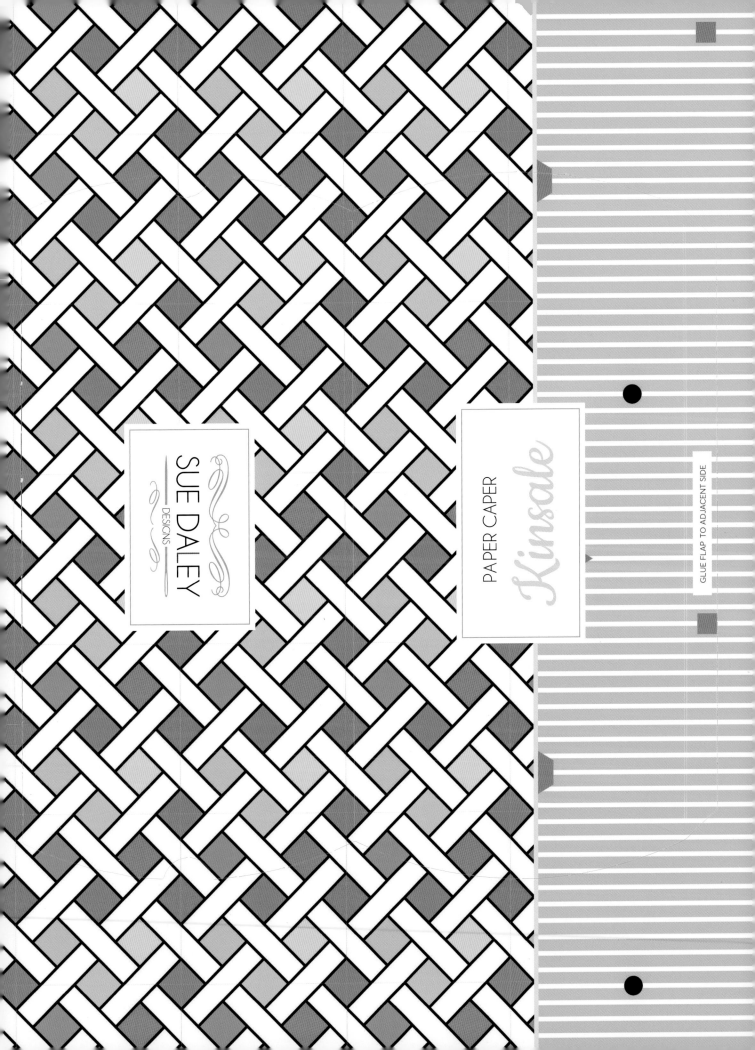

SUE DALEY
DESIGNS

PAPER CAPER
Kinsale

GLUE FLAP TO ADJACENT SIDE

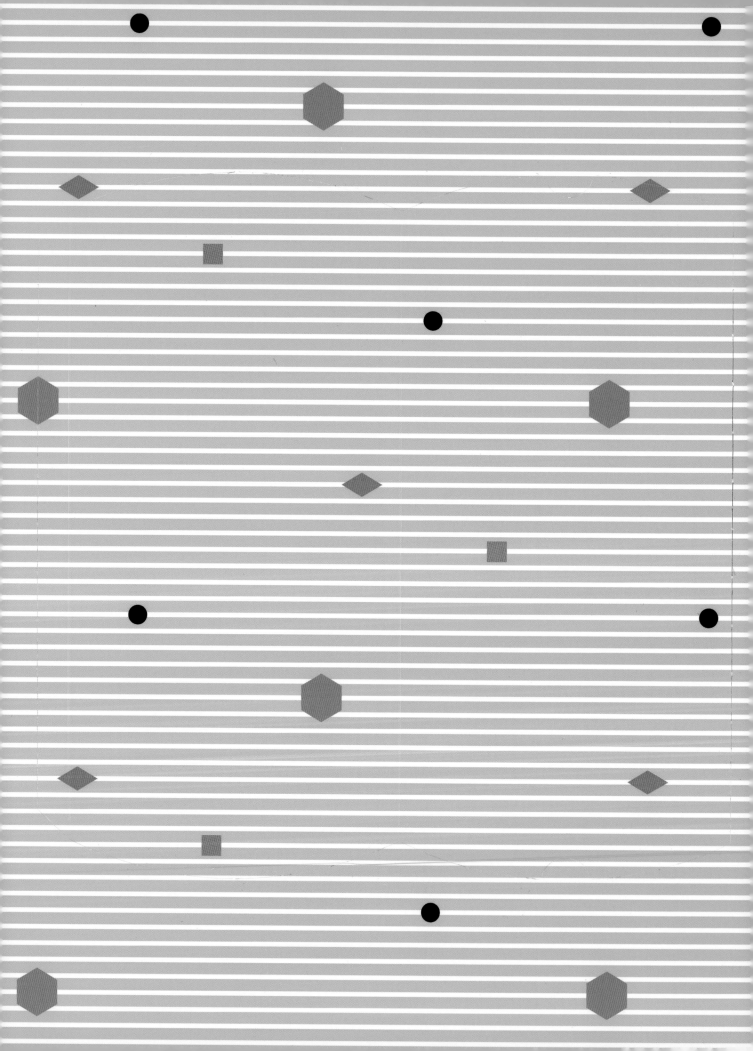

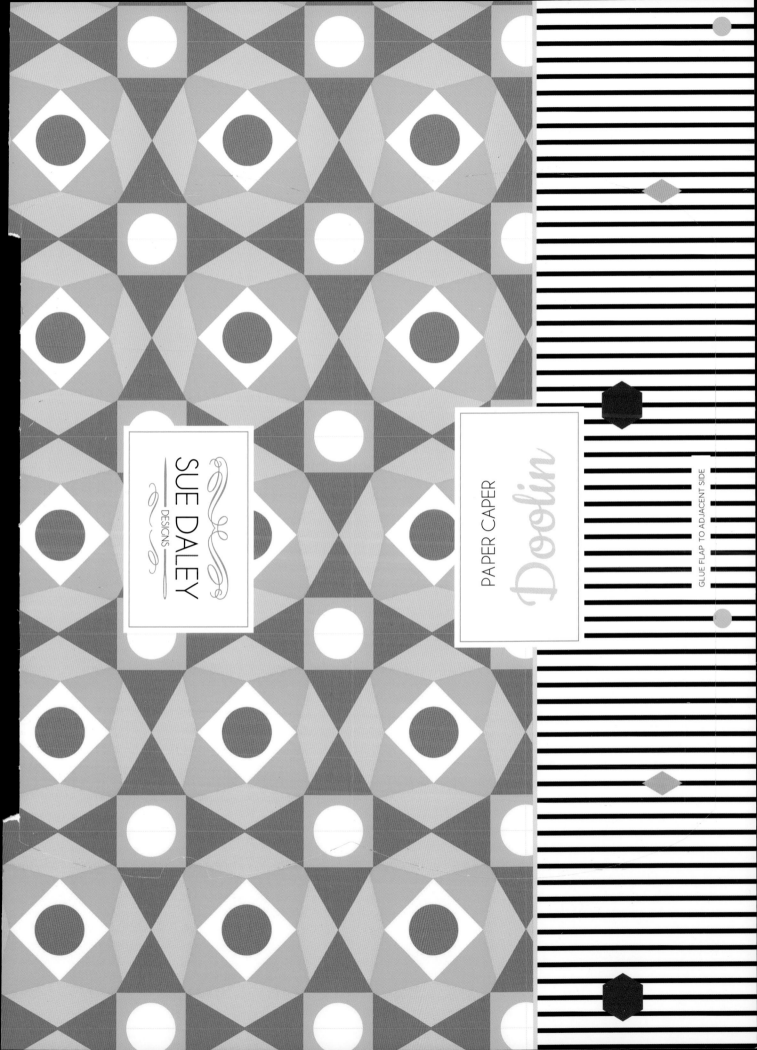

SUE DALEY
DESIGNS

PAPER CAPER
Doolin

GLUE FLAP TO ADJACENT SIDE

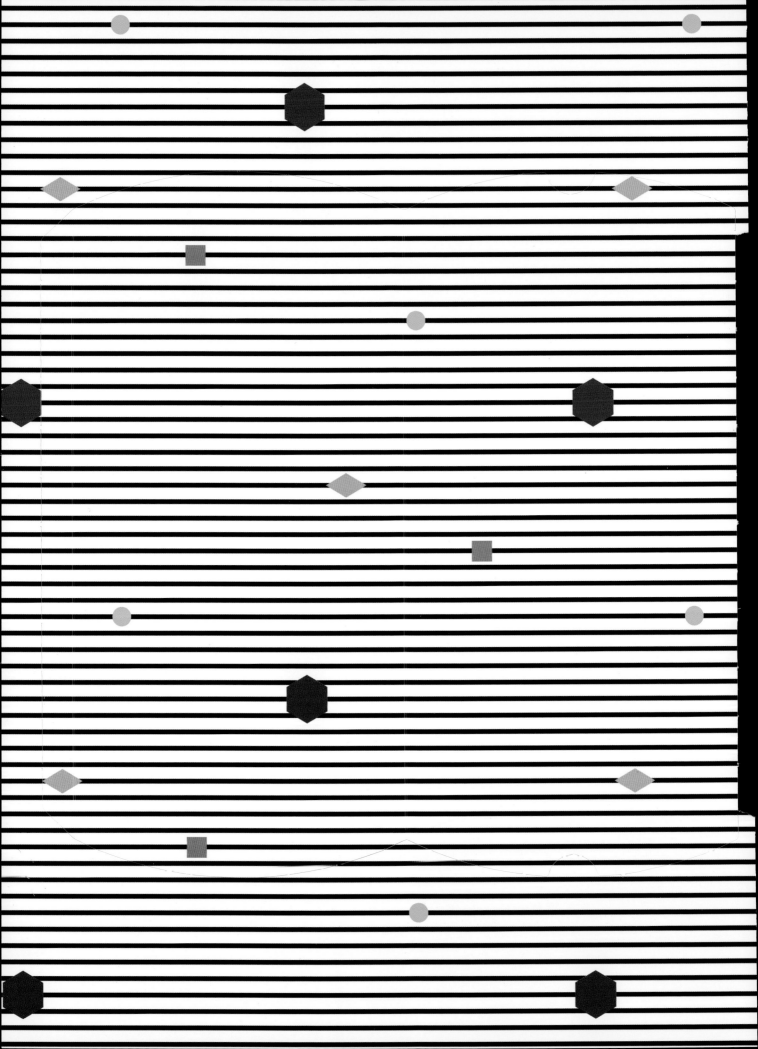

WICKLOW

WICKLOW

E

C

B

D

A

A

^

E

A

A

D

B

A

A

C

A

A

A

C

A

B

A

D

A

E

A

A

D

A

A

E

Circle

B

C

WICKLOW

WICKLOW

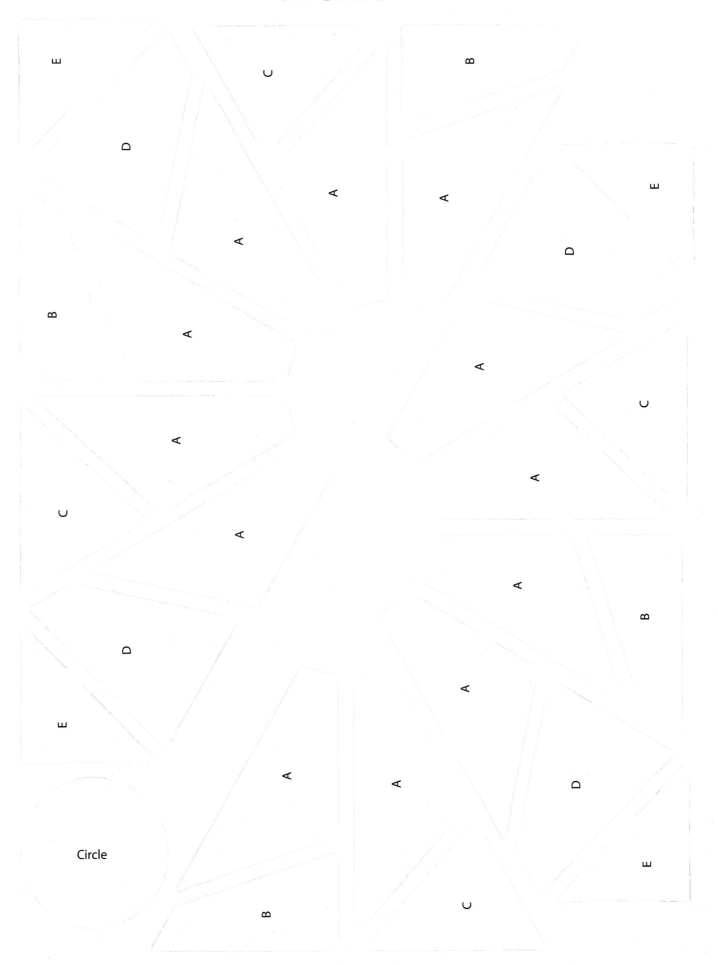

Circle

SHANNON

B

B

B

B

B

B

B

A

A

A

B

B

B

B

B

D

A

A

D

B

B

B

B

B

A

A

A

B

B

B

B

B

B

B

B

C

B

A

C

B

B

B

B

C

C

A

SHANNON

B

B

B

B

B

B

A

A

A

B

B

B

B

B

D

A

A

D

B

B

B

B

B

B

A

A

A

B

B

B

B

B

B

C

B

B

B

C

B

B

B

A

C

C

SHANNON

B

B

B

B

B

B

A

A

A

B

B

B

B

B

B

D

A

A

D

B

B

B

B

B

A

A

A

A

B

B

B

B

B

C

B

A

C

B

B

B

B

A

C

C

C

SHANNON

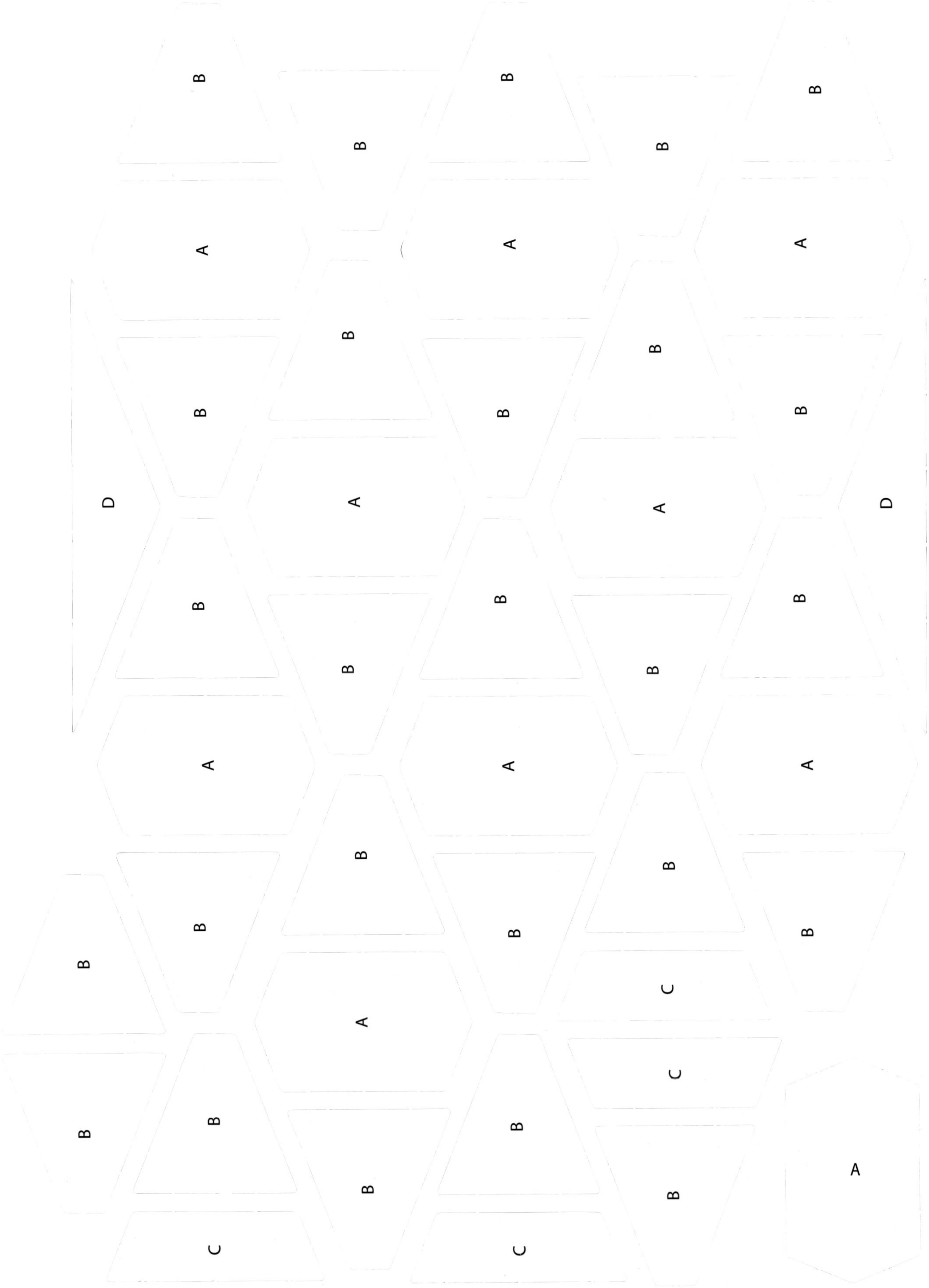

B

B

B

B

B

B

B

A

A

A

B

B

B

B

B

D

A

A

D

B

B

B

B

B

B

A

A

A

B

B

B

B

B

B

C

A

C

B

B

B

B

A

C

C

C

SHANNON

A · A · A · A

B · B · B

A · A · A

B · B · B

B · A · B

KINSALE

KINSALE

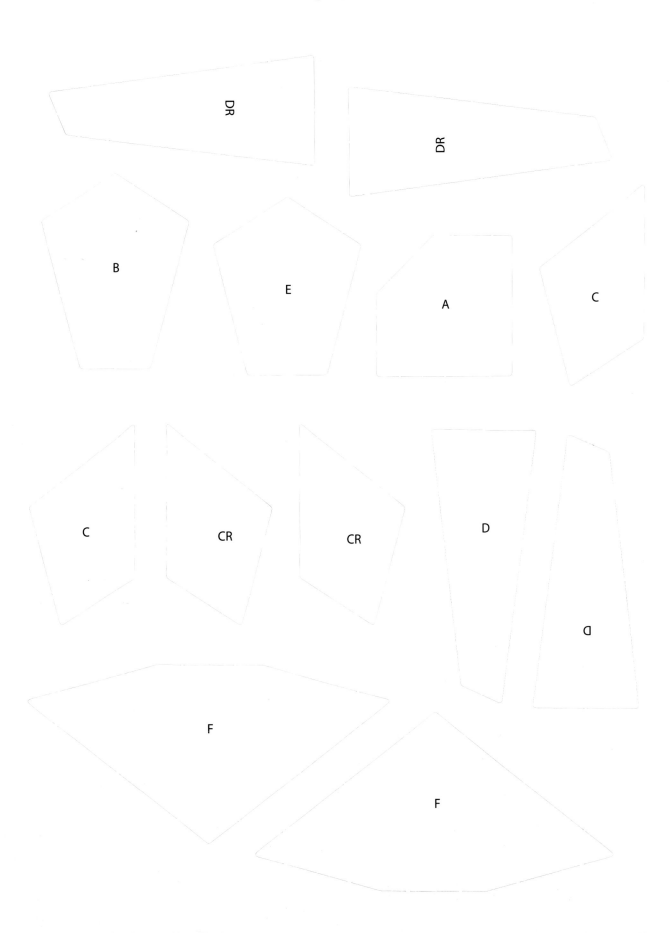

KINSALE

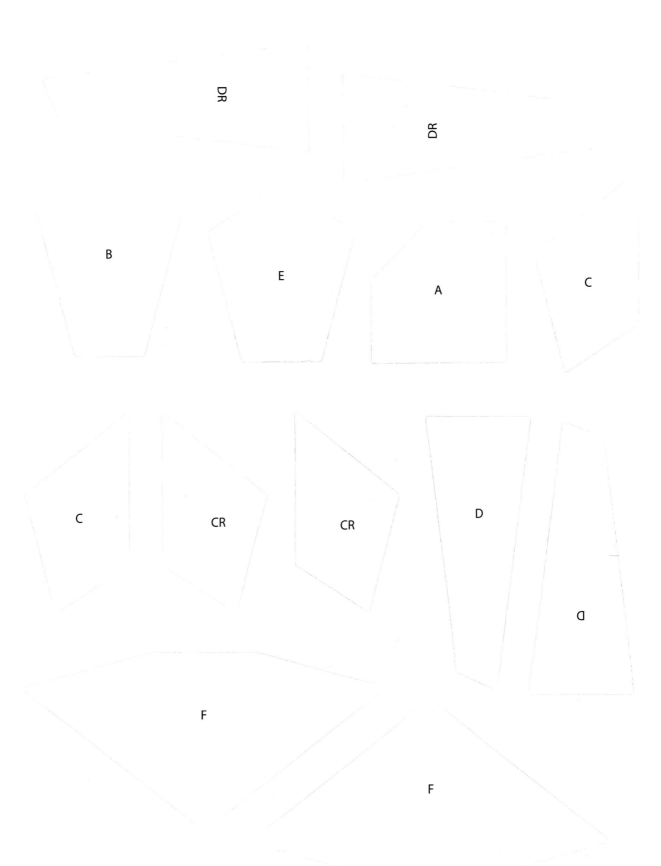

KINSALE

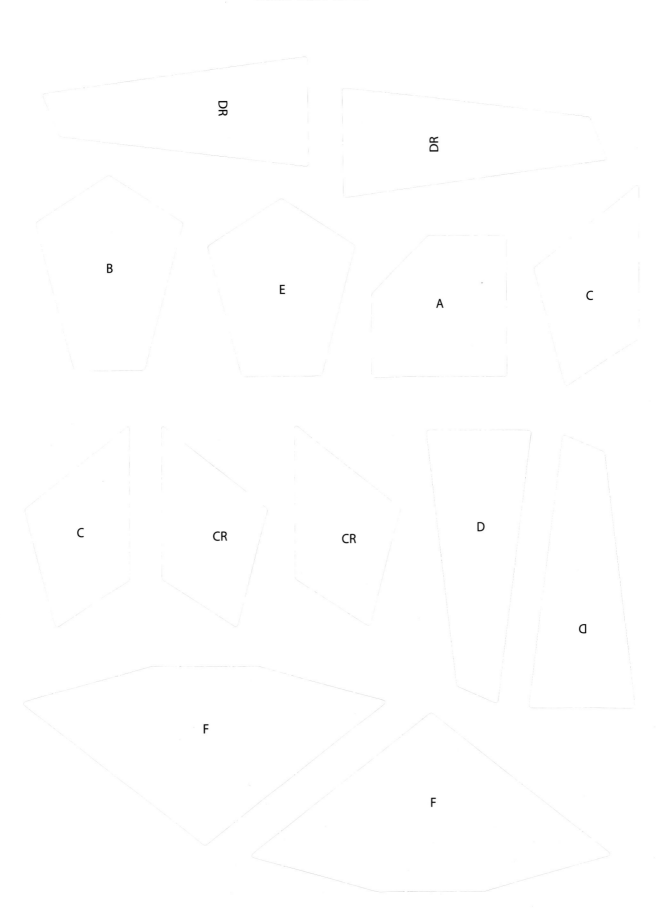

DOOLIN

B

C

C

A

B

D

D

A

B

B

B

B

A

B

B

A

B

A

A

B

B

A

C

C

A

A

A

DOOLIN

B

C

C

A

B

D

D

A

B

B

A

B

B

B

A

B

A

A

B

B

A

C

C

A

A

A

DOOLIN

B

C

C

A

B

D

D

B

B

A

B

B

B

A

B

A

A

B

C

C

A

A

WATERFORD

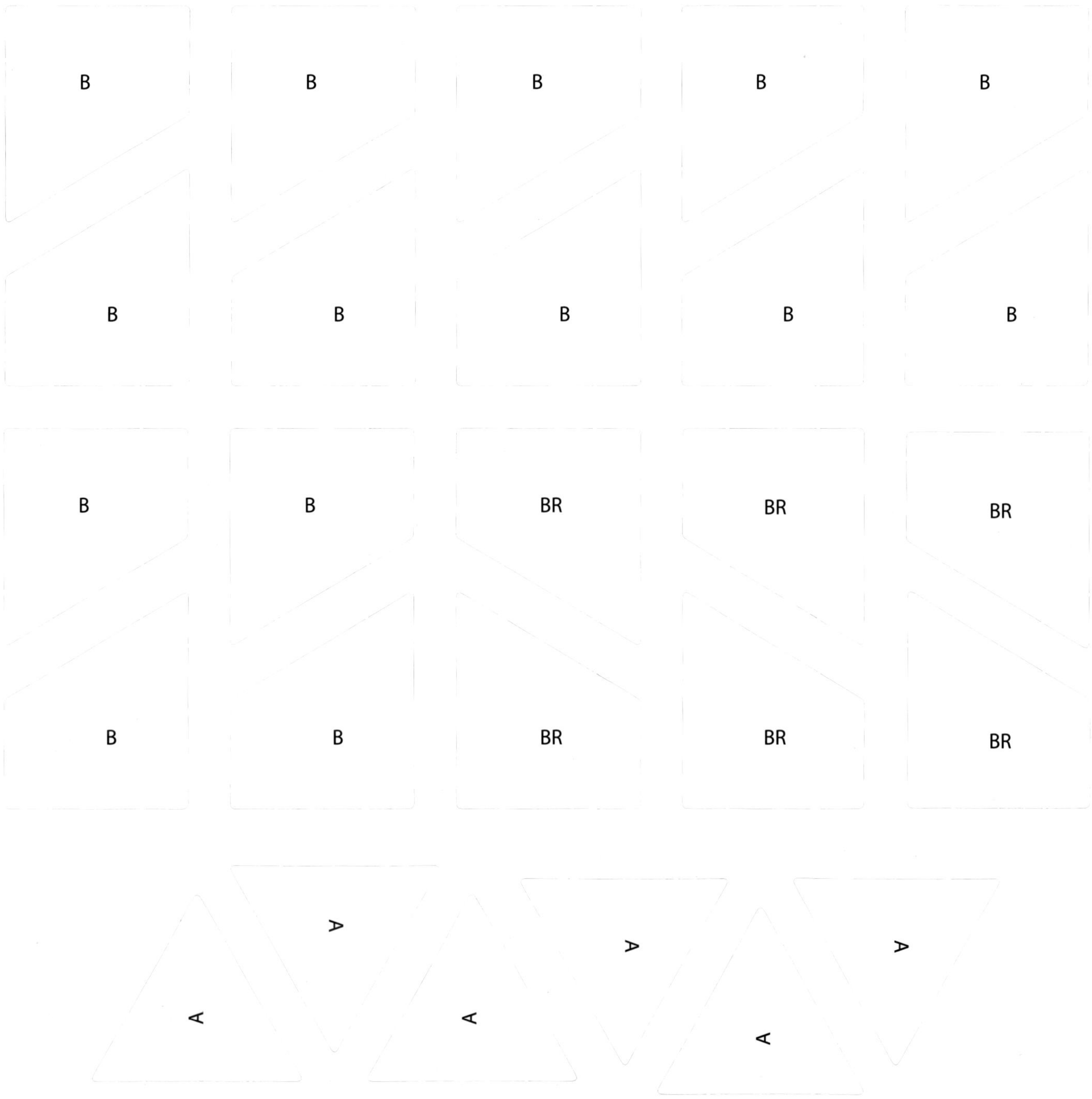

B   B   B   B   B

B   B   B   B   B

B   B   BR   BR   BR

B   B   BR   BR   BR

A   A   A

A   A   A

WATERFORD

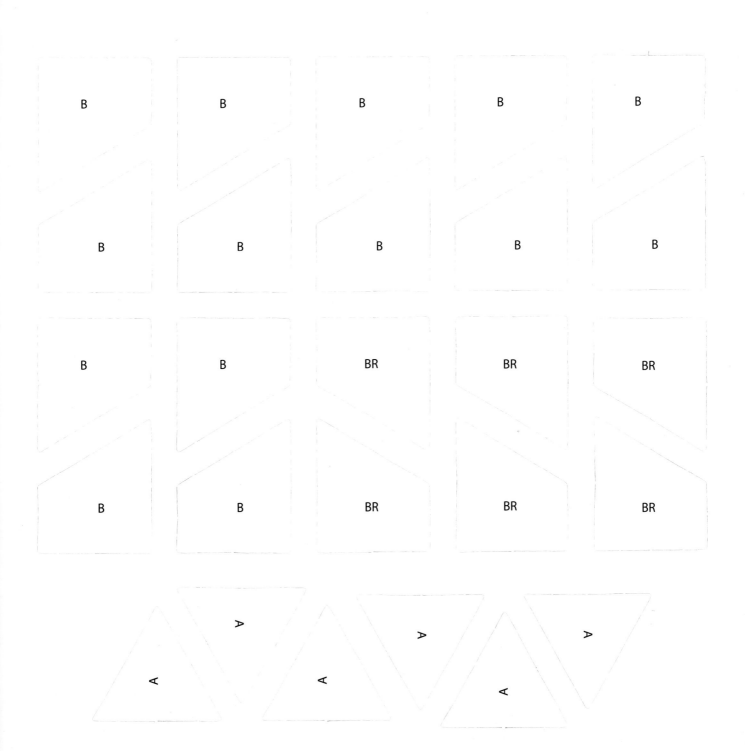

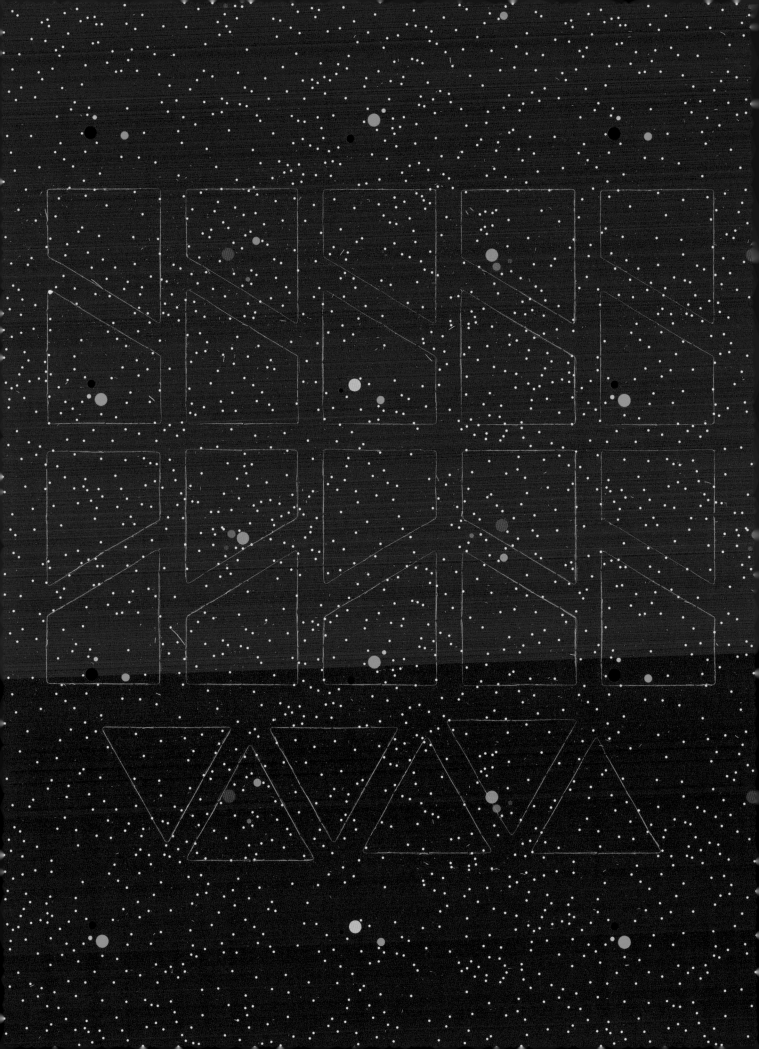

WATERFORD

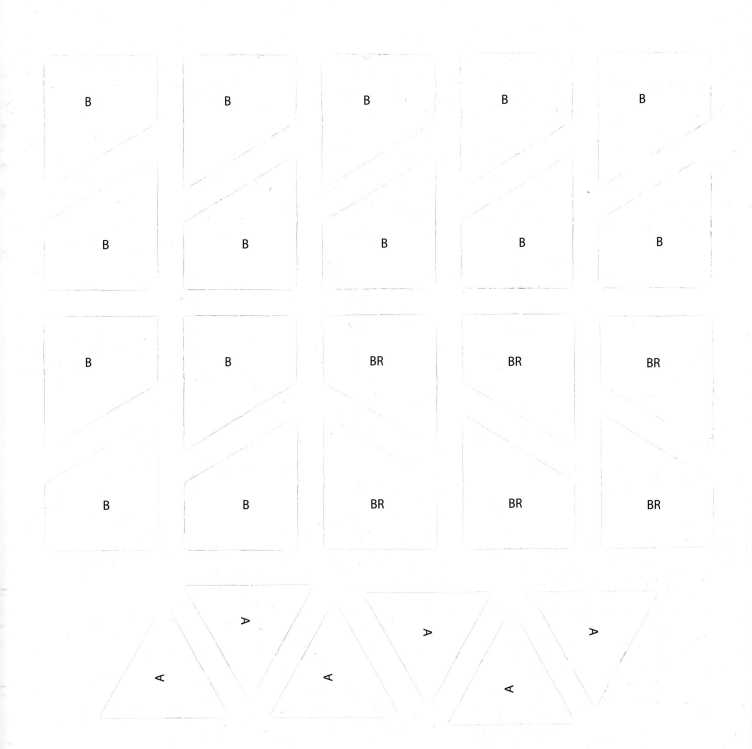

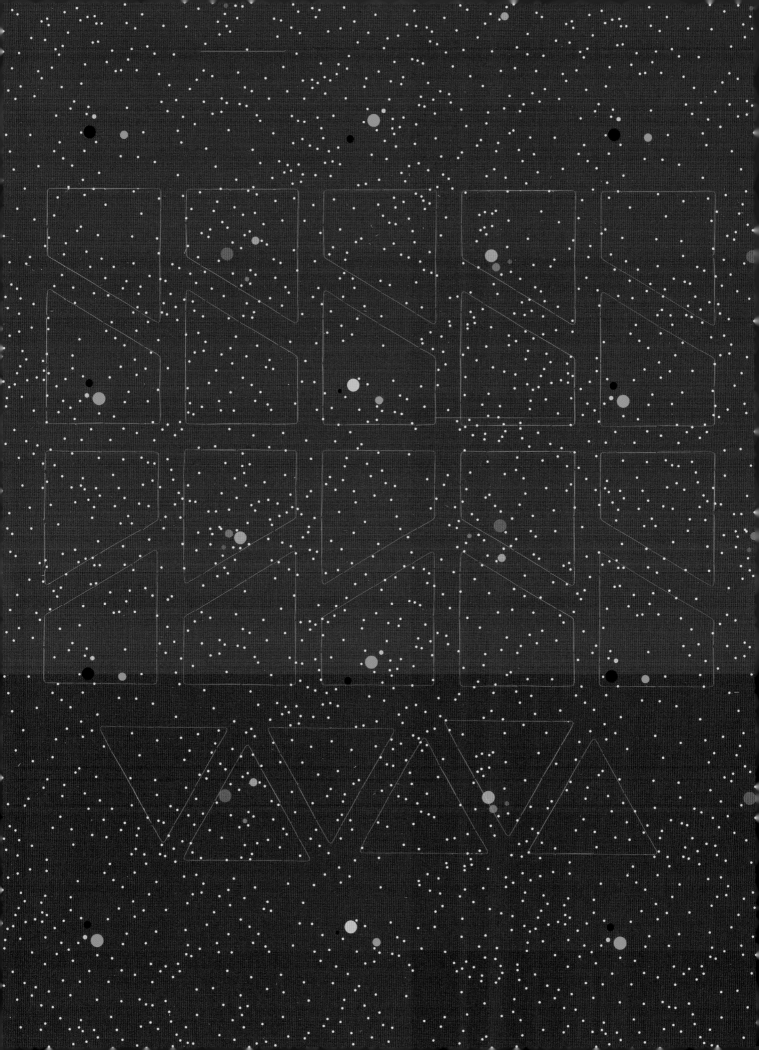

CASHEL

CASHEL

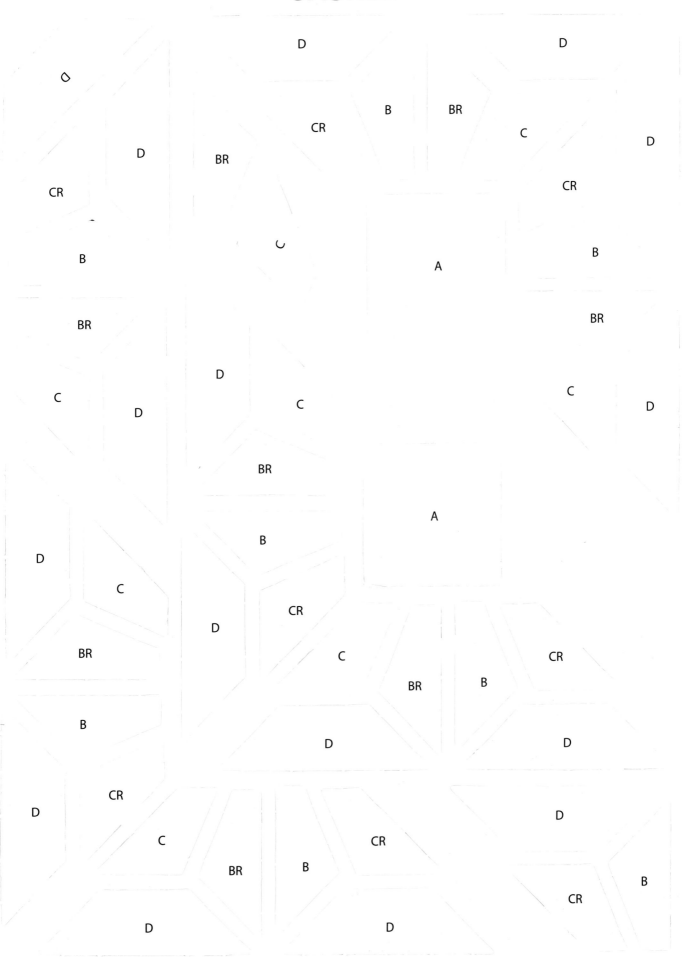

CASHEL

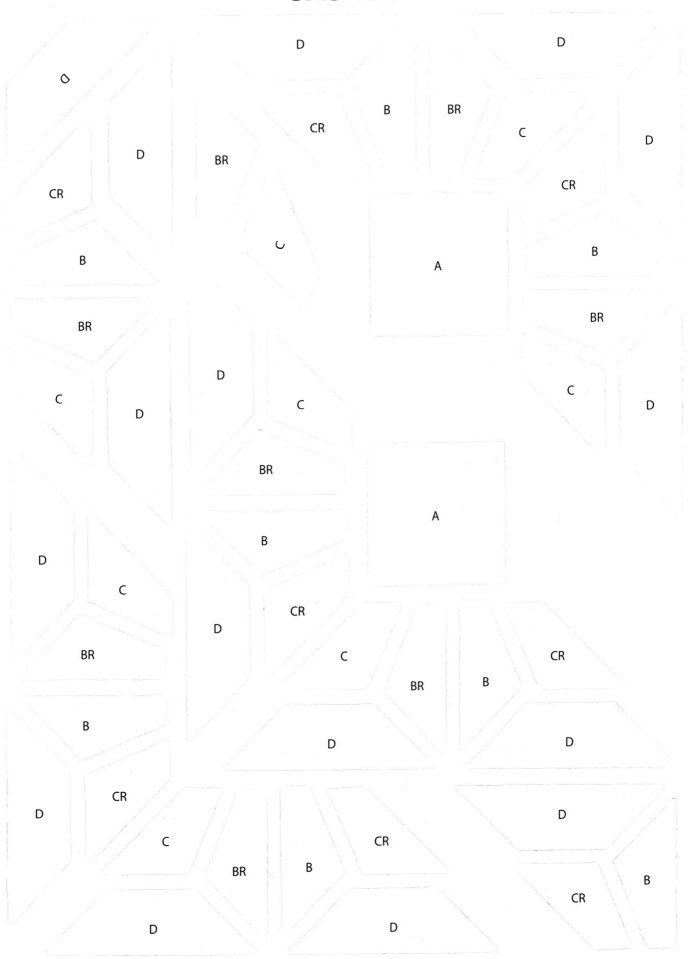

CASHEL

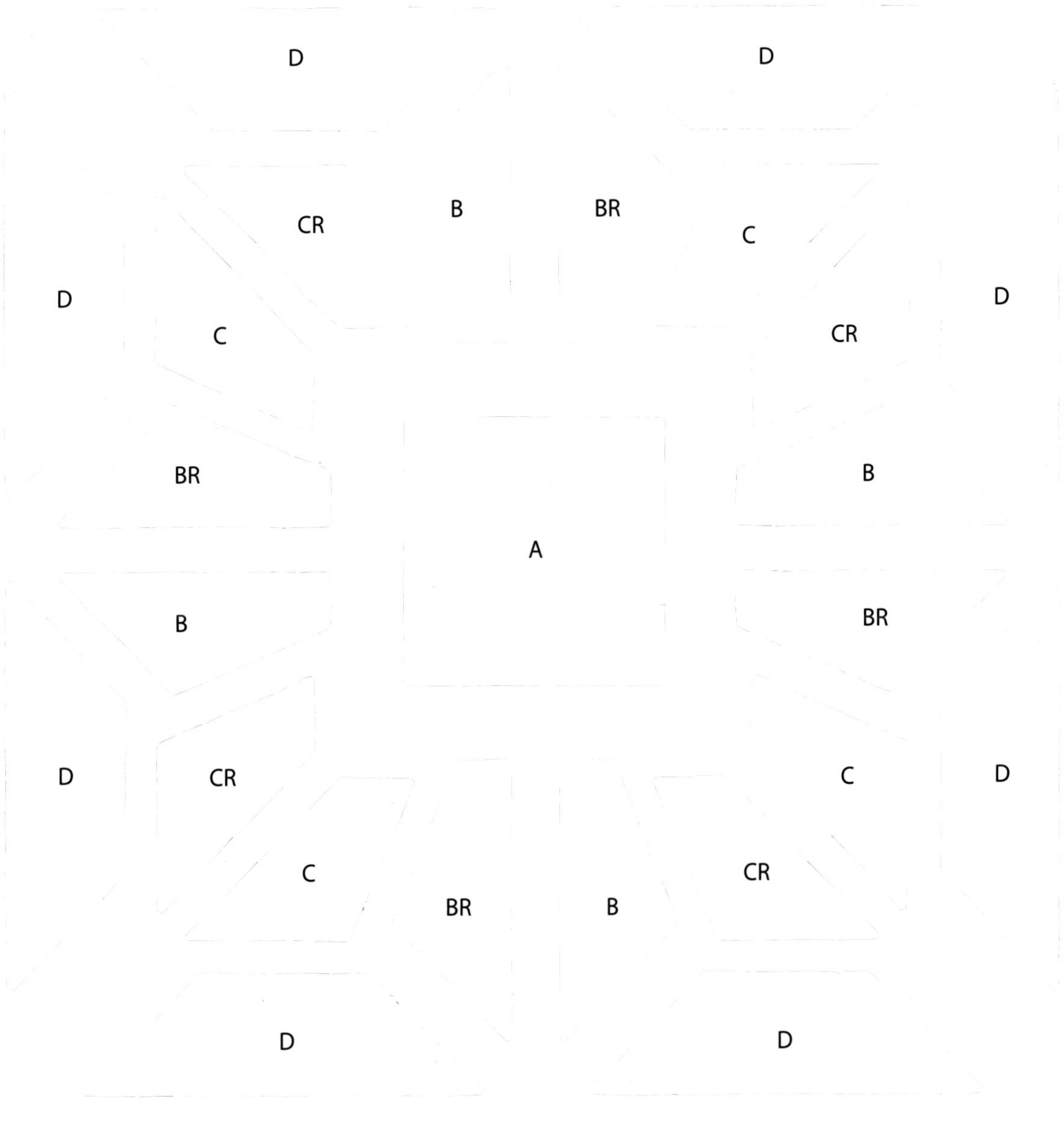

D   D

CR   B   BR   C

D   C   CR   D

BR   B

A

B   BR

D   CR   C   D

C   CR

BR   B

D   D

CASHEL

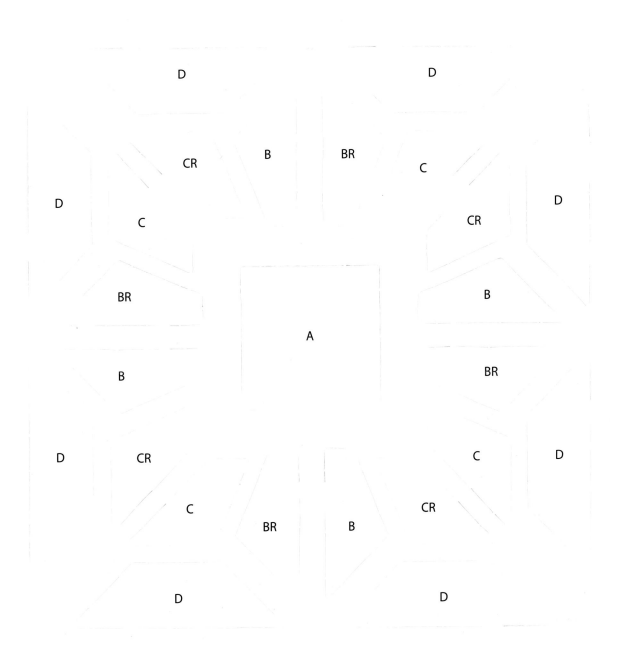

CASHEL

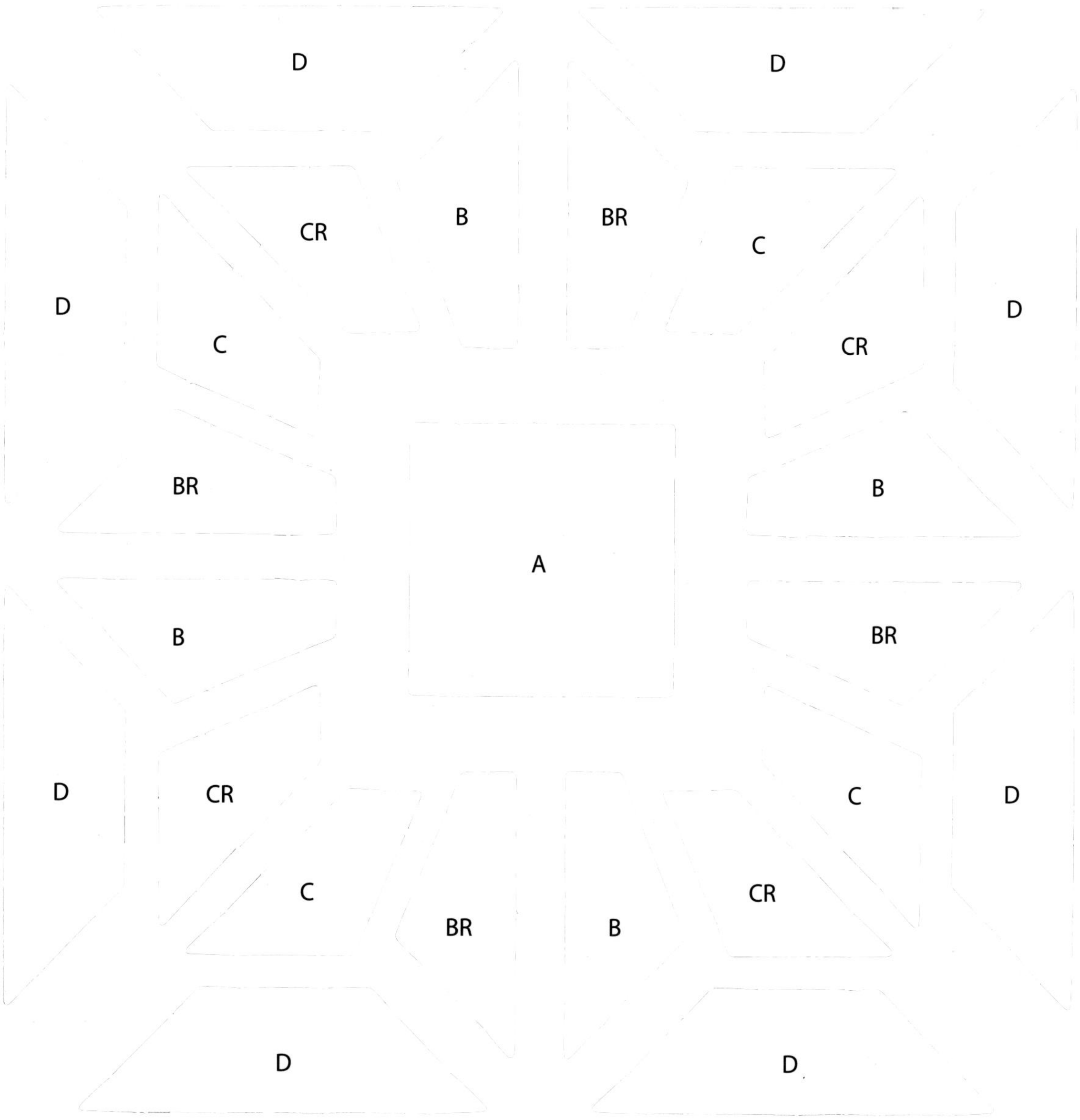

D

D

CR

B

BR

C

D

D

C

CR

BR

B

A

B

BR

D

CR

C

D

C

CR

C

BR

B

D

D

BONUS SHAPES

B

B

B

B

B

B

A

A

A

B

B

B

B

B

B

D

A

A

A

D

B

B

B

B

B

A

A

A

BONUS SHAPES

BONUS SHAPES

B

B

B

B

B

B

A

A

A

B

B

B

B

B

B

D

A

A

A

D

B

B

B

B

B

B

A

A

A

BONUS SHAPES